Modern Dining *for Life*

Cover and Food photographs by Justin Grierson

Copyright © 2009 Marshall Cavendish International (Asia) Private Limited

Published by Marshall Cavendish Cuisine
An imprint of Marshall Cavendish International
1 New Industrial Road, Singapore 536196

All rights reserved

No part of this publication may be reproduced, stored in a retrieval system
or transmitted, in any form or by any means, electronic, mechanical, photocopying, recording or otherwise, without the prior permission of the copyright owner. Request for permission should be addressed to the Publisher, Marshall Cavendish International (Asia) Private Limited, 1 New Industrial Road, Singapore 536196. Tel: (65) 6213 9300 Fax: (65) 6285 4871
E-mail: genref@sg.marshallcavendish.com
Online bookstore: http://www.marshallcavendish.com

The Intellectual Property of Daniel Green, its brand expression "The Model Cook" and "Green's Twist" and all related indicia presented herein are owned and exclusively managed by Astra Worldwide Limited, Hong Kong. For all enquiries, please contact vivien.lee@astraonair.com

Limits of Liability/Disclaimer of Warranty: The Author and the Publisher of this book have used their best efforts in preparing this book. The parties make no representation or warranties with respect to the contents of this book and are not responsible for the outcome of any recipe in this book. While the parties have reviewed each recipe carefully, the reader may not always achieve the results desired due to variations in ingredients, cooking temperatures and individual cooking abilties. The parties shall in no event be liable for any loss of profit or any other commercial damage, including but not limited to special, incidental, consequential, or other damages.

Other Marshall Cavendish Offices:

Marshall Cavendish Ltd. PO Box 65829, London, EC1P 1NY, UK • Marshall Cavendish Corporation, 99 White Plains Road, Tarrytown NY 10591-9001, USA • Marshall Cavendish International (Thailand) Co Ltd. 253 Asoke, 12th Flr, Sukhumvit 21 Road, Klongtoey Nua, Wattana, Bangkok 10110, Thailand • Marshall Cavendish (Malaysia) Sdn Bhd, Times Subang, Lot 46, Subang Hi-Tech Industrial Park, Batu Tiga, 40000 Shah Alam, Selangor Darul Ehsan, Malaysia

Marshall Cavendish is a trademark of Times Publishing Limited

National Library Board Singapore Cataloguing in Publication Data

Green, Daniel.
Modern dining for life / Daniel Green. – Singapore: Marshall Cavendish Cuisine, c2009.
p. cm
Includes index.
ISBN-13 : 978-981-261-744-6

1. Low-fat diet – Recipes. 2. Cookery. I. Title.

TX714
641.56384 -- dc22   OCN456479415

Printed in Singapore by Times Printers Pte Ltd

Daniel Green

Modern Dining
for Life

To mum and dad with love:
Now I will never need to forget my football boots!

contents

Stylish Dining For Healthwise Foodies	6
A Food Safety Reminder from Daniel	8
Green's Twist:	
Smart Changes for Healthier Cooking & Eating Habits	10
Starters and Appetisers	12
Vegetables and Salads	42
Rice, Pasta and Noodles	56
Meat and Poultry	72
Fish and Seafood	94
Desserts	120
Green's Menu Planner	133
Basic Recipes	134
Weights & Measures	142
Index of Recipes	143

stylish dining for healthwise foodies

The recipes in this book are very special to me. I have cooked from this book for friends, family, dinner parties, fine dining events at premium hotels around the world, for the prestigious Royal KLM Dutch Airlines and now, for you.

Over the years, I have always been determined to prove to the culinary world that just low-fat, healthy food does not need to be poor in presentation. I want to show you that such food can be displayed well and will look as good as any dish that is served in fine dining establishments. I also want to show how easy it is to create the "wow" factor in food without one having any formal culinary experience.

Today's restaurant food is more about food that is well-executed and presented. I want to show you my Green's twist interpretation of the restaurant food of this time. There is nothing nicer than having seafood on an ice tier tray in Paris, sushi in Japan, or fusion cuisine in Australia, and now I would like to share with you how easy it is to recreate the same effect in the comfort of your home.

One of the best things about my work is the fact that I get to travel to many countries. In my experience, only very few cuisines stand out in their fantastic appeal—healthy and tasty, yet presented in a style that is also pleasing on the eye. Countries like Australia, Japan, Hong Kong and Thailand would top the lists for me.

My life is my daughter, Eleanor, and my wife, Jane, and food plays a great part in our lives. We have travelled together with my in-laws and my parents, and enjoyed dining at many fine restaurants around the world.

Food brings people together, is always a process of discovery and makes an interesting topic of conversation. I love the aspect of Chinese culture that believes feeding people is a show of love, and I hope you will enjoy cooking for your loved ones the recipes in this book.

I also want to encourage people who have stopped cooking, to try my recipes—they are really very easy!

Thanks for buying my cookbook and making it as a part of your culinary experience at home with your loved ones.

Happy cooking!

a food safety reminder from Daniel

Outbreaks of food borne illnesses occur frequently today, so it is good to know the causes and how it can be prevented in the home. One of the most common forms of food borne illnesses is food poisoning. It is typically caused by eating food that has been poorly handled, stored or cooked.

The symptoms of food poisoning vary depending on the amount of the contaminated food eaten, as well as the contaminants, but the most common symptoms include nausea, vomiting, diarrhoea and stomach cramps.

Daniel Green sharing a light moment with Chef Nobu, Executive Chef of Sheraton Towers, Singapore.

Wash Your Hands
Wash your hands thoroughly with soap and warm water before preparing food and after handling raw meats, poultry, fish and unwashed vegetables.

Store Food Well
Use separate cooking utensils when preparing or storing raw foods and packaged ready-to-eat foods. Wash all cooking utensils and storage containers well before using.

Keep raw meats, poultry and fish refrigerated at all times.

Thawing and Reheating Food

Defrost frozen meats, poultry and fish thoroughly before cooking, and avoid re-freezing food that has been thawed. When reheating food, cook it until it is boiling or steaming hot. When storing cooked food for use later, cover and refrigerate it once it is no longer steaming.

Plan Your Shopping

Purchase hot, chilled or frozen foods only towards the end of your shopping trip, so you can bring them home as quickly as possible. When transporting hot, chilled and frozen food, keep them separate. Once you are home, place the chilled and frozen foods immediately into the refrigerator or freezer. When shopping, avoid the juices from meat, poultry and fish leaking into your other purchases such as ready-to-eat foods or vegetables.

Wash Fruit and Vegetables Well

Rinse fruit and vegetables well before using or consuming them.

Check Your Purchases

Avoid choosing products in damaged or dented packaging, or products that are bruised, mouldy or discoloured.

Watch What You Eat

Avoid eating foods that have been left out for some time. Chilled foods should be kept chilled at 5°C (40°F) or lower and hot foods should be kept hot at 60°C (140°F) or hotter.

If you are ever in doubt about the safety of a food item, avoid eating it and throw it out.

Green's Twist:
smart changes for healthier cooking & eating habits

As an advocate for healthy eating, people often ask me how they can lose weight. There are many kinds of diets that one can go on, and these may work for some, but for others, these diets may not be practical or sustainable.

Through my personal experience, I have found that making small changes over time will make big differences, and it will be something you can maintain without too much of a struggle. Here are some tips which I have personally found useful.

The recipes in this book also feature one or more tweaks which I call "Green's Twist" for a healthier approach to enjoying good food.

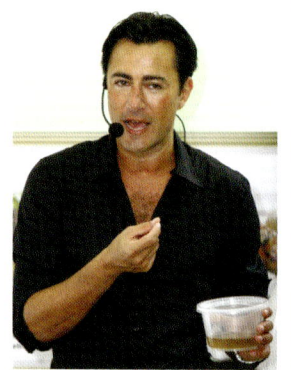  

Daniel Green launches "Tangs Culinary Moments" by Tangs, a leading fashion lifestyle retailer in Singapore.

Tips For Eating Out

Order a dish that is mainly made up of protein. Ask to substitute carbohydrates (such as potato, rice and pasta) with vegetables instead. Restaurants generally serve them in generous portions, so don't worry about going away hungry.

Choose your restaurant based on the cuisine they serve. For example, Japanese and Thai cuisines have a wide variety of healthy dishes.

Always ask for the dressing for your salad to be on the side. Restaurants tend to pile on creamy dressings such as Ranch and Caesar, which have high fat content. Alternatively, ask for vinaigrette or oil-based dressings instead.

Tips For Losing Weight

Forget fad diets; the best way to lose weight is to sustain a healthy diet. By cutting out food that is high in fat content, you'll have better and longer-lasting results.

Don't snack late at night; whatever food you may eat will be "wasted" energy. If you must, take fruit juice or yoghurt as a snack instead.

I do not agree with people who say "don't weigh yourself"; on the contrary, weighing yourself makes you more aware of how much physical activity you are doing, and what you eat every day.

Don't feel guilty about treating yourself a little during the weekend! As long as you lead a balanced diet and healthy lifestyle, enjoy food for what it is!

Tips For Healthy Cooking

Try brushing your food with a little oil before cooking, instead of using oil to cook the food. Better yet, try cooking without oil. Invest in good-quality non-stick cookware which will minimise the need for oil. You'll be amazed at the results!

When cooking meats such as beef or lamb, place the meat over a bed of rock salt, then cook in the oven. The salt absorbs the fat from the meat but keeps it moist and juicy.

I've said it before, and I'll say it again: say no to deep-frying, cooking with butter, cream and cheese, on a daily basis!

starters & appetisers

Crab & Avocado Tower 13

Spicy Chilli Calamari 14

Japanese Tuna Tartare 16

Salmon & Avocado Wrap 18

Scallops on Red Wine 20

Prawns with Tomato Coulis 22

Bean Curd Guacamole 24

Salad with Pumpkin Seeds 26

Caesar Salad 28

Salad with Everything 30

Bread Dips, Two Flavours 32

Asparagus Raft 34

Soup de Poisson 36

Tomato & Basil Soup 38

Sweet Corn & Lemon Grass Soup 40

Some ingredients are like a match made in heaven, and crab and avocado is one such example. This dish makes a classic and elegant starter.

crab & avocado tower
Serves 4

140 g (5 oz) fresh or premium tinned crabmeat

Juice of 1 lemon

3 Tbsp extra-virgin olive oil

Rock salt to taste

Crushed black pepper

2 large, ripe avocados, pitted

4 spring onions (scallions), finely chopped

A handful of fresh basil leaves

Frisée salad leaves

Herb oil (page 136)

- Marinate crabmeat with half the lemon juice, olive oil, salt and pepper. Set aside.
- Chop avocado finely and place it in a bowl. Adding remaining lemon juice. Shred basil leaves and add to avocado, then add spring onions and mix well.
- Place a round ring cutter on a serving plate. Place some avocado mixture in to create the base, then top with marinated crabmeat. Press down firmly to compact the avocado and crabmeat before releasing the ring. Repeat step for remaining crabmeat and avocado mixture.
- Top with salad leaves and drizzle over herb oil and serve immediately.

spicy chilli calamari
Serves 4

Coated in a simple batter of breadcrumbs, then lightly fried and dressed in a spicy, piquant sauce, this calamari dish certainly beats the usual deep-fried, battered versions served in most restaurants!

2 eggs

4–6 slices day-old white bread

$1^{1}/_{2}$ medium-sized squid tubes, cleaned and cut into evenly-sized rings

2 Tbsp olive oil

Spicy Tomato Sauce

2 Tbsp olive oil

$^{1}/_{2}$ cup tomato sauce

1 Tbsp sun-dried tomato paste (process some sun-dried tomatoes in a blender with some olive oil)

2 garlic cloves, peeled and crushed

3 bird's eye chillies, chopped

- Prepare spicy tomato sauce. Heat oil in a pan, then add remaining ingredients. Let mixture simmer over low heat for 3–4 minutes, then transfer to a blender and process until smooth. Set aside.

- In a bowl, beat eggs and set aside. Place bread in a blender and process into crumbs. Place breadcrumbs on a plate and set aside.

- Heat oil in a large pan over high heat. Dip a handful of squid rings into beaten eggs, then coat with bread crumbs. Fry squid rings for 3–5 minutes in small batches, so as not to overcrowd the pan and lower the cooking temperature.

- Toss calamari in spicy tomato sauce and serve immediately.

japanese tuna tartare
Serves 4

Tuna tartare is served in all the finest modern restaurants and it is so simple to make. The trick is to present this in a spectacular fashion and grab the attention of all your guests! Use sashimi-grade tuna and you are all set!

400 g (14$^{1}/_{3}$ oz) sashimi-grade tuna, finely chopped
2 Tbsp chopped spring onions (scallions)
2 Tbsp black or white sesame seeds
Juice of 2 limes
1 tsp chopped pickled ginger
2 Tbsp sesame oil
2 Tbsp light soy sauce
1 tsp prepared wasabi paste
Herb oil (page 136)

- Place tuna, spring onions, sesame seeds, lime juice, ginger and sesame oil in a bowl and mix well.
- In a separate bowl, mix soy sauce and wasabi paste, then add to tuna and toss well.
- Place an oblong, square or round pastry cutter on a serving plate. Spoon in about a quarter of the marinated tuna and press down firmly to compact. Gently remove pastry cutter. Repeat step to make 4 servings.
- Drizzle herb oil decoratively and serve immediately.

salmon & avocado wrap

Serves 4

If you worry about eating carbohydrates but love sushi, then this one is for you. I use a fat-free cream cheese; if this is not available in your home town, then use a fromage frais with no fat, or a little plain yoghurt.

4 nori seaweed sheets

8 slices of smoked salmon

1 avocado, peeled and pitted

8 Tbsp fat-free cream cheese, or use plain fat-free yoghurt

- Place seaweed sheets on a clean work surface. Spread 2 Tbsp cream cheese evenly over each sheet, then divide and place slices of smoked salmon over cream cheese.
- Slice avocado into 2.5-cm (1-in) thick strips lengthwise, and lay across the seaweed. Starting from one side, roll seaweed up tightly.
- Slice rolls into half at an angle before serving. Serve immediately.

scallops on red wine

Serves 4

Scallops are very light in flavour, so the strength of the red wine really compliments the dish. Many top restaurants spend a lot of time making a red wine reduction, but I have found some shortcuts to doing that, without compromising any flavour.

1 Tbsp olive oil

6 shallots or 1 small white onion, peeled and finely chopped

1 clove garlic, peeled and crushed

375 ml (12 fl oz / 1$\frac{1}{2}$ cups) red wine

100 ml (3$\frac{1}{2}$ fl oz) vegetable stock (page 134)

12 large, fresh scallops

- Heat oil in a pan over medium heat. Add shallots or onion and fry for 5 minutes.
- Add garlic, then wine and stock. Bring to the boil and simmer for about 20 minutes until the sauce is reduced and thickened. Turn off heat and leave it to sit for 10 minutes, then reheat until thickened.
- Heat a nonstick pan until very hot. Brush scallops with olive oil, then sear for 1 minute on each side.
- Spoon some red wine sauce on each serving plate, followed by scallops. Serve immediately.

prawns with tomato coulis

Serves 4 to 6

This dish is inspired by Spanish tapas, or finger food that goes with light drinks and beer.

12 tiger prawns, cooked

1 Tbsp fresh dill

1 Tbsp fresh parsley

1 Tbsp lemon juice

1 lemon, grated for zest

Salt to taste

Crushed black pepper to taste

1 Tbsp olive oil

1 clove garlic, peeled and crushed

Tomato Coulis

$1/2$ cup tomato sauce

4 Tbsp olive oil

$1/2$ clove garlic, peeled and crushed

- Make tomato coulis. Combine all ingredients in a pan and leave to simmer for 3–4 minutes.
- Peel prawns and discard shell and heads. Chop dill and parsley finely, then place in a mixing bowl together with prawns, lemon juice and zest, salt, pepper and garlic.
- Drizzle tomato coulis over and serve immediately.

bean curd guacamole

Serves 4 to 6

The combination of bean curd and avocado provide a healthy, nutritious alternative to regular guacamole, which is high in fat.

3 ripe avocados, peeled and pitted
Juice of 1 lime
A handful of chopped fresh coriander (cilantro)
225 g (8 oz) silken bean curd, drained
1 small red bird's eye chilli
4 spring onions (scallions), chopped

- Combine all ingredients except spring onions in a food processor and process until slightly chunky. Add spring onions and mix in well.
- Serve guacamole as a dip with tortilla chips, or with toasted bread slices as a canapé.

salad with pumpkin seeds

Serves 4

I have had some of the best salads in southern France, where they are often served with poached eggs. This salad is no exception, and the pumpkin seeds add crunch and sweet nuttiness. Paired with a classic salad dressing, this salad is simple but delicious.

Mixed salad leaves, enough for 4 people

3–4 slices of bread, cut into $1/2$-cm ($1/4$ in) cubes

125 g ($1/2$ cup) pumpkin seeds

500 ml (16 fl oz / 2 cups) water

250 ml (8 fl oz / 1 cup) white vinegar

4 eggs

Dressing

1 cup olive oil

$1/4$ cup white vinegar

2 Tbsp Dijon mustard

- Make dressing. Combine ingredients in a mixing bowl and mix well. Set aside. Brush bread cubes with a little olive oil, then grill for a few minutes or until golden brown.
- In a large mixing bowl, toss salad leaves with pumpkin seeds, dressing and croutons. Divide into 4 serving portions and set aside.
- To poach eggs, place two parts water to one part white vinegar in a pan. Bring to a rolling boil. Crack on egg into the water and poach for 2 minutes. Remove egg gently with a slotted spoon and place in a bowl of cold water to stop the cooking process. Repeat to cook the remaining eggs.
- Top each salad portion with a poached egg and serve immediately.

caesar salad

Serves 4

Nothing beats a classic Caesar salad as a starter, or even as a full meal if you add grilled skinless chicken to make it more substantial!

1 large head of Romaine (cos) lettuce
4–5 anchovy fillets
1 hard-boiled egg, peeled

Dressing

2–3 canned anchovy fillets
2 tsp Dijon mustard
1 egg yolk
A dash of Worcestershire sauce
Juice of $1/2$ lemon
4-6 Tbsp extra-virgin olive oil

- Slice lettuce and place in a large bowl.
- Combine ingredients for dressing in a blender and process until smooth. Pour over lettuce and mix well.
- Top lettuce with anchovy fillets. Using a vegetable grater, grate egg over the salad. Serve immediately.

salad with everything

Serves 4

This has to be the most flavourful salad I have made to date. Every bite has an explosion of texture and taste!

Mixed salad leaves enough for 4 people

½ red onion, peeled and sliced very finely

1 avocado, peeled, pitted and finely chopped

12 cherry tomatoes, halved

3 strips of bacon, fried until crisp without using oil and coarsely chopped

125 g (½ cup) pistachio nuts

125 g (½ cup) toasted sunflower seeds

Dressing

250 ml (8 fl oz / 1 cup) olive oil

Juice of 1 lemon

1 egg yolk

6–8 Sun-blushed Tomatoes (page 135)

2 Tbsp Dijon mustard

1 Tbsp chopped fresh parsley

- Make dressing by combining all ingredients together.
- Combine salad ingredients in a large mixing bowl, then pour dressing over and toss well. Serve immediately.

bread dips, two flavours

Serves 4

These dips are great alternatives to butter, and a lot more exciting in flavour too! Versatile and easy to prepare, any sort of bread would go wonderfully with them.

Garlic and Pepper-infused Oil

6-8 Tbsp extra virgin olive oil

1 clove garlic, peeled and thinly sliced

8–10 whole peppercorns

A pinch of rock salt (optional)

Olive Tapenade

1 tin of pitted black olives

Salt to taste

Crushed black pepper to taste

1 Tbsp Dijon mustard

1 clove garlic, peeled

6–8 fresh basil leaves

4 Tbsp olive oil

Juice of 1 lemon

1 Tbsp capers

- To make garlic and pepper-infused oil, simply combine olive oil, garlic and peppercorns and leave for at least 1 hour. Sprinkle your bread with a little rock salt before dipping it into the infused oil, if desired.
- To make olive tapenade, combine all ingredients in a blender and process until fine.

asparagus raft

Serves 4

The nutty flavour and crunchy texture of asparagus goes perfectly with the smooth, silky avocado broth.

24–30 medium-size asparagus spears
1 ripe avocado, peeled and pitted
125 ml (4 fl oz / $^1/_2$ cup) vegetable stock (page 134)
Freshly ground black pepper to taste
55 g (2 oz) salmon roe
Herb oil (page 136)

- Cut asparagus into equal sizes. Taking about 4 stalks at a time and starting at the tips, cut off around 7.5 cm (3-in). Using one of the tips as a measure, take the same amount off remaining stalks. Discard uneven leftovers.
- Add asparagus to a pan of boiling water. Cook for 3 minutes, then run under ice-cold water to stop the cooking process, to retain colour and crunchiness.
- Place avocado and stock in a blender and blend until smooth. Season well with black pepper.
- To serve, put a few spoonfuls of avocado broth on the base of serving plate. Make a raft with asparagus on 2 levels, with the first lined up one way, and the next going the other way. Top with salmon roe. Drizzle herb oil over and serve immediately.

soup de poisson

Serves 4 to 6

This soup is served in restaurants throughout France and it is an absolute favourite of mine. Make it more substantial by adding lots of seafood and serve it as a main dish.

Trimmings (heads, skin and bones) of 4 medium-sized fish (sea bass or salmon)

1 small can of tomato purée

4 cloves garlic

A handful of chopped parsley

1 bay leaf

A sprig of thyme

Salt to taste

Pepper to taste

2 small red chillies

1 litre (32 fl oz / 4 cups) water

Toast

1 thin French baguette, sliced into rounds

Olive oil for drizzling

A handful of chopped chives

$1/4$ tsp rock salt

- Place all ingredients in a stockpot. Cover and simmer over low heat for 1 hour.
- Remove and discard fish trimmings. Use a handheld blender and process soup until smooth.
- Prepare toast. Place baguette on a baking tray and drizzle with olive oil. Sprinkle with chives and rock salt. Toast until lightly crisp.
- Ladle soup into bowls and top with 1–2 rounds of toast. Serve immediately.

tomato & basil soup

Serves 4

This dish is great for dinner parties as it goes well with most other dishes and can be made well in advance.

2 Tbsp olive oil

1 Tbsp minced garlic

1/2 cup chopped onions

5 cans of tomatoes, about 800 g (28 oz) each, plus their juices

2/3 cup fresh basil leaves, blended into a purée

2 tsp sugar

1/8 tsp cayenne pepper

2 Tbsp red wine vinegar

1 litre (32 fl oz / 4 cups) vegetable stock (page 134)

- Heat olive oil in a large pan and fry garlic and onions for about 5 minutes or until soft over low heat.
- Add all other ingredients and simmer for about 20 minutes. Using a handheld blender, process soup until smooth.
- Ladle into bowls and garnish as desired.

sweet corn & lemon grass soup

Serves 8

Light, subtle flavours is the theme of this delicious soup. The lemon grass gives off a bracing, uplifting scent while cooking!

10–12 stalks lemon grass

8–10 ears sweet corn

2 Tbsp olive oil

1 large onion, peeled and finely chopped

1 clove garlic, peeled and crushed

2 litres (64 fl oz / 8 cups) vegetable stock (page 134)

- Peel away the tough outer leaves of the lemon grass to get to the tender white part. Trim ends and chop finely. Set aside.
- Pull away the husk from sweet corn, then pull out the silk and discard. Using a knife, cut off corn kernels and place in a bowl.
- Heat oil in a large stock pot. Add onion and cook for 2–3 minutes.
- Add lemon grass, garlic and corn kernels. Stir for a minute, then add stock. Lower heat and leave soup to simmer for 20–25 minutes.
- Serve soup as is, or use a handheld blender and process soup until smooth before serving. Serve hot.

vegetables

Green's Energiser 43

Roasted Baby Aubergines 44

Roasted Edamame with Garlic 46

Roasted Vegetables 48

Taboule 50

Wasabi Mash 52

Sun-dried Tomato Mash 54

I had a dish like this in a very trendy organic restaurant in Los Angeles and it was fantastic. Sometimes, the body craves nothing but greens, and this is an absolutely fantastic way to eat them. Be amazed at the boost of energy you will get!

green's energiser

Serves 4

½ bulb of garlic

3-4 cups broccoli

3-4 cups kale

2 cups sugar snap peas

1 avocado, peeled, pitted and chopped into small chunks

½ cup pistachio nuts

½ cup dried cranberries

½ cup roasted edamame beans

3 Tbsp extra-virgin olive oil

Rock salt to taste

- Place garlic on a sheet of aluminium foil. Drizzle some olive oil over garlic, then roast in the oven at 180–200°C (350–400°F) until garlic is soft and fragrant. Remove from oven and leave to cool slightly, then gently squeeze garlic cloves from their skins. Set aside.
- Bring a pot of water to the boil. Blanch broccoli, kale and sugar snap peas for 2 minutes, then remove place under cold running water, or in a basin of cold water to arrest the cooking process and help the vegetables retain their colour. Drain well.
- Combine garlic, blanched vegetables and remaining ingredients in a large mixing bowl and mix and season well. Serve immediately.

roasted baby aubergines

Serves 4

These sweet, delicious aubergines are fantastic when roasted. They can be a side dish and served with any main course

6 baby aubergines (eggplants/brinjals)
2 Tbsp olive oil
A pinch of rock salt
A splash of white truffle oil (optional)
Fresh herbs like rosemary sprigs (optional)

- Preheat oven to 220°C (440°F).
- Slice aubergines into half lengthwise, starting from the stalk. Place aubergine halves in a large bowl and toss with oil and salt, coating them well.
- Place aubergine halves, cut side facing up, on a sheet of aluminium foil. Place on a roasting pan and roast for 20–25 minutes. Halfway through roasting time, turn aubergines over once.
- Serve immediately, garnished with fresh herbs, if desired.

roasted edamame with garlic

Serves 4

Edamame are great on their own, but roasting them with garlic really adds a new dimension of flavour! Great as a side dish or starter.

2 cups fresh soy beans (*edamame*), removed from pods
4 Tbsp olive oil
6 cloves garlic, peeled
Salt to taste
Crushed black pepper to taste

- Preheat oven to 230°C (450°F).
- Combine beans, garlic and oil and toss well. Season with salt and pepper, then transfer to a roasting pan or baking tray
- Place in the oven about 12 minutes, tossing mixture once or twice. Serve by itself, or as a side with main dishes.

roasted vegetables

Serves 6

I love roasted vegetables—it is such an easy-to-make dish and a winner all round. Great as a side accompaniment to main dishes and filling enough to be a main dish, you can add some bacon or ham if you don't have to go vegetarian.

- 1 butternut squash, peeled and deseeded
- 1 sweet potato, peeled
- 3-4 carrots, peeled
- 3-4 zucchinis (courgettes)
- 12 button mushrooms
- 12 brussels sprouts
- 4 slices of thick white bread, cut into 1-cm ($1/2$-in) cubes
- 4 Tbsp olive oil
- 3 cloves crushed garlic
- 3 sprigs of fresh rosemary leaves
- 1 sprig of fresh thyme
- Salt to taste
- Pepper to taste

- Preheat oven to 220°C (440°F).
- Prepare vegetables. Cut butternut, sweet potato, carrots and zucchini into 1-cm ($1/2$-in) cubes. Slice mushrooms and brussel sprouts into half.
- Place vegetables and bread cubes in a roasting pan. Add olive oil, garlic, herbs and salt and pepper. Toss well, making sure vegetables and bread cubes are well coated. Place in the oven to roast for 30–40 minutes, tossing vegetables occasionally.
- Serve hot.

taboule

Serves 4

Taboule is a wonderful middle Eastern dish, and is the perfect vegetarian recipe that's quick and easy to toss together at the last minute. Great on a summer's day with a glass of chilled white wine.

250 g (9 oz) cous cous
4 vine-ripened tomatoes
½ cucumber
½ red onion, peeled and finely chopped
1 cup fresh spinach, cooked
1 bunch spring onions, sliced
45 g (1½ oz) fresh parsley
1 lemon, grated for zest
6 Tbsp olive oil
2 Tbsp lemon juice
1 clove of garlic, peeled and crushed
Salt to taste

- Bring some water to the boil. Place cous cous into a large bowl and pour boiling water over, until grains are covered. Cover with a plate and let it stand for 5 minutes. Break grains up with a fork. Set aside.
- Finely dice tomatoes, cucumber, onion and spinach. Slice spring onions and chop parsley until fine.
- Add vegetables and lemon zest to cous cous. Whisk together olive oil, lemon juice and garlic with salt to taste and drizzle over taboule before serving.

wasabi mash

Serves 4

I love mashed potatoes, but they are hardly what one would call trendy restaurant food. Now, with an Asian twist due to the addition of wasabi, they have become fashionable again!

4 large potatoes, peeled and quartered

$1/2$ cup low-fat (skim) milk

3 Tbsp olive oil

1 tsp salt

1 tsp wasabi powder, mixed with 2 Tbsp water, or use 1 Tbsp prepared wasabi paste

- Bring a pot of water to the boil. Place potatoes in for 20–25 minutes or until tender. Remove and drain.
- Transfer potatoes to a blender. Add milk, olive oil, salt and wasabi powder or paste mix and blend until smooth.
- To serve, use two tablespoons to scoop and shape mash into quenelles as shown in the picture. Garnish with some freshly chopped coriander, if liked.

sun-dried tomato mash

Serves 4 to 6

Gone are the days when mash was lumpy and full of butter. Jazz up your meal with this Mediterranean-style sun-dried tomato mash instead!

4 large baking potatoes
1/2 cup skim (non-fat) milk
3 Tbsp olive oil
8–10 sun-dried tomatoes in olive oil, drained and sliced
12–16 black olives, pitted
1 tsp salt
6–8 spring onions (scallions), chopped

- Peel potatoes, then cut them into quarters. Bring a pot of water to the boil, then place potatoes in to cook for 20–25 minutes or until potatoes are tender.

- Drain potatoes and transfer to a food processor. Add milk and olive oil and process until smooth and free of lumps. Transfer to a mixing bowl and mix in remaining ingredients.

- Garnish with spring onions. Serve mash hot.

pasta, noodles & rice

Pasta with Trio of Mushrooms 57

Truffle Risotto 58

Edamame Risotto 60

Shanghai Noodles 62

Sesame Soba Noodles 64

Egg Noodles with Chicken & Vegetables 66

Soba Noodle Soup 68

Green Tea Noodles with Salmon & Avocado Mousse 70

This is a very simple and elegant pasta to make. The truffle oil and pine nuts add a woody, nutty aroma and flavour to the dish, making this a pure delight to eat!

pasta with trio of mushrooms

Serves 4

1 packet of dried fettuccine
1/2 cup dried porcini mushrooms, chopped
3 Tbsp olive oil
1 onion, peeled and finely chopped
1 cup fresh shiitake mushrooms, chopped
2 cups button mushrooms, chopped
3 cloves garlic, peeled and crushed
1 cup of roasted pine nuts
A handful of fresh basil leaves
1 Tbsp truffle oil

- Cook your pasta according to instructions on the packet. While pasta is cooking, soak dried mushrooms in 1/2 cup of boiling water to reconstitute them for 5 minutes. Reserve the soaking water for use later.
- When pasta is cooked to al dente, drain, place in a large bowl or container and keep warm.
- Heat 1 Tbsp olive oil in a large pan over medium heat. Fry onion until fragrant. Add shiitake and button mushrooms and stir-fry for 3–4 minutes, then add garlic, porcini mushrooms and about 3–5 Tbsp of the soaking water. Stir-fry mixture for another minute or so, then remove from heat.
- Toss pasta with stir-fried mushrooms, pine nuts, basil leaves and truffle oil. Serve immediately.

truffle risotto

Serves 4

Truffles are terribly expensive, and rarely seen in domestic kitchens. However, you can recreate the flavour and aroma with truffle oil at less than half the cost!

6 Tbsp truffle oil
1 large onion, peeled and finely chopped
2 large carrot, finely chopped
2 cloves of garlic, peeled and crushed
6 shiitake mushrooms, sliced thinly
10–14 button mushrooms, sliced thinly
1 litre (32 fl oz / 4 cups) vegetable stock (page 134)
300 g (11 oz) arborio rice
1 glass of white wine (optional)
A handful of chopped fresh parsley (optional)

- Heat 3 Tbsp of truffle oil in a pan over medium heat. Add onions and cook for 2–3 minutes, followed by carrots and garlic. Stir ingredients for a minute, then add mushrooms and cook for another minute. Meanwhile in a separate pot or pan, bring stock to the boil.
- Add arborio rice to pan with mushrooms and mix well. Add wine, if using, and leave to simmer for a minute. Add a ladle of stock at a time, stirring continuously for 20 minutes until creamy and tender. Add remaining truffle oil in the last minute of cooking.
- Garnish risotto with some fresh chopped parsley, if liked, and serve immediately.

edamame risotto

Serves 4

Edamame risotto is truly a match made in heaven. The sweet nuttiness of the beans go perfectly with the smooth, creamy texture of the arborio rice. This will make an elegant main course.

4 Tbsp olive oil
1 large onion, peeled and chopped finely
2 cloves garlic, peeled and crushed
1 litre (32 fl oz / 4 cups) vegetable stock (page 134)
300 g (11 oz) of arborio rice
1 glass of white wine (optional)
1 cup soy beans (*edamame*), removed from pod
2 Tbsp sesame seeds
1 Tbsp sesame oil
A handful of finely chopped parsley

- Heat oil in a frying pan over medium heat. Fry onions for 2–3 minutes or until fragrant, then add garlic and fry for 1 minute. Meanwhile, bring vegetable stock to a boil in a separate pot.

- Add arborio rice and stir to mix well with onion and garlic. Add white wine, if using, and leave to simmer for 1 minute, then add soy beans. Vegetable stock should be boiling by now; add a ladle at a time while stirring continuously for 20 minutes. Stir in sesame seeds.

- Dish out, drizzle with sesame oil and garnish with parsley before serving. For a fancier presentation, pack risotto into a oblong or rectangular pastry cutter on a plate and press down firmly to compact into a round shape.

shanghai noodles

Serves 4 to 6

I've served this to both adults and children alike and they love it, the children especially. The nuttiness of sesame oil is enhanced through the tahini paste and peanut butter—not typically Shanghainese, I know—but delicious nevertheless!

250 g (9 oz) dried soba noodles
1 Tbsp peanut butter
1 Tbsp tahini paste
2 carrots, peeled and cut into strips
2 Tbsp sesame oil
2 Tbsp sesame seeds
1 Tbsp light soy sauce
6 spring onions (scallions), sliced

- Cook soba noodles according to the instructions on pack. Soba noodles typically do not need more than 5–7 minutes to cook, depending on the thickness of each strand. When noodles are cooked, drain and place in a mixing bowl.
- Add remaining ingredients and toss with noodles, mixing well. Serve immediately.

sesame soba noodles

Serves 4 to 6

My entire extended family loves this dish, especially my dad and daughter, Eleanor. It's a really quick and easy dish to whip up, and great to have on a chilly day.

250 g (9 oz) dried soba noodles

1 Tbsp olive oil

6–10 fresh shiitake mushrooms, sliced (if fresh mushrooms aren't available, use dried mushrooms and reconstitute them in hot water for 30 minutes)

2 Tbsp sesame oil

1 Tbsp light soy sauce

2 Tbsp sesame seeds

$1/2$ cup peanuts, roughly chopped or processed in a blender

$1/2$ cup coconut milk (use low-fat coconut milk if possible)

1 small red chilli, deseeded and chopped

6–8 spring onions (scallions), chopped

- Cook soba noodles (page 62). When noodles are cooked, drain and place in a mixing bowl.

- Heat olive oil in a pan over medium heat. Cook mushrooms for about 3–5 minutes, then add noodles and sesame oil, soy sauce, sesame seeds, peanuts, coconut milk and chilli. Stir-fry noodles for another minute, then remove from heat.

- Dish noodles out and garnish with spring onions. Serve immediately.

egg noodles with chicken & vegetables

Serves 4

This quick stir-fry is a popular Chinese restaurant favourite. However, the noodles are often very oily and fattening as well. My version uses minimal oil but yields fantastic results. Try it!

2 skinless chicken breasts, sliced into 2.5-cm (1-in) pieces

450 g (1 lb) mixed vegetables (broccoli, cauliflower, zucchini, mushrooms and carrots), chopped

300 g (11 oz) cooked egg noodles

1 Tbsp oyster sauce

2 cloves garlic, peeled and crushed

1 red chilli, finely chopped

- Heat about 1–2 Tbsp oil in a wok over medium-high heat. Fry chicken strips for 3-5 minutes until cooked, then add mixed vegetables and stir to mix well. Add 125 ml (4 fl oz / $1/2$ cup) water and cook for 3–5 minutes.
- Add noodles, oyster sauce, garlic and chilli and toss ingredients to mix everything well. Allow mixture to simmer for another minute, then remove from heat.
- Dish out and serve immediately.

soba noodle soup

Serves 6

There are trendy Asian noodle outlets opening up all over the place nowadays. I have spent much time in Asia, and I love their noodles in all forms. This recipe is great with lots of fresh vegetables; feel free to improvise with them!

1 litre (32 fl oz / 4 cups) water

2 chicken stock cubes

16 large fresh prawns, peeled

4 cups cooked soba noodles (page 62)

4 Tbsp oyster sauce

A dash of cayenne pepper to taste

1 Tbsp sesame oil

3 Tbsp sesame seeds

8–10 button mushrooms

4–6 bundles of Chinese cabbage (*pak choy*)

- Combine water and stock in a pot and bring to the boil. In a wok, heat a little oil over high heat and fry prawns until they turn pink.
- Add noodles, oyster sauce, pepper, sesame oil and seeds and toss well to mix. Cook for a minute, then add mushrooms, Chinese cabbage and stock. Cook for 3–5 minutes and taste and adjust seasoning, if required.
- Dish out into serving bowls and serve immediately.

green tea noodles with salmon & avocado mousse

Serves 6

There is something very Zen-like, peaceful and elegant about this dish. The subtle flavour of green tea, creamy avocado and fresh salmon come together in the unlikeliest of ways. Serve this at a dinner party; your guests will love the presentation as well!

4 salmon fillets, about 200 g (7 oz), skinned

1 avocado, peeled and pitted

1/2 cup vegetable stock (page 138)

Salt to taste

Crushed black pepper to taste

2 Tbsp chopped fresh basil leaves

450 g (1 lb) green tea noodles, cooked according to instructions on packet

1 Tbsp olive oil

- Heat a pan over medium heat. Place salmon fillets in and pour in enough water to cover. Bring to the boil, then remove from heat and cover pan for 10 minutes.
- Meanwhile, place avocado, vegetable stock, salt, pepper and basil leaves in a blender and blend until smooth. Set aside.
- Toss noodles with olive oil, then divide into 4 portions. Place salmon over noodles and serve, with avocado mousse on the side.

meat

Chicken with Kaffir Lime Leaf & Cauliflower 73

Beef Yakitori 74

Beef Stew 76

New York Strip Steaks with Red Wine & Pomegranate Sauce 78

Sesame Steaks 80

Venison Steaks with Red Wine & Mushroom Sauce 82

Lamb with Wasabi Crust 84

Herb-crusted Rack of Lamb with Parsnip Purée 86

Seared Foie Gras with Rocket Leaves & Figs 88

Calf's Liver on Wasabi Mash 90

Chopped Liver 92

I love this fusion of East and West. It is so tasty with plain rice, and the kaffir leaves perfumes and lifts the dish in an amazing way!

chicken with kaffir lime leaf & cauliflower

Serves 4

1 large cauliflower head, chopped into florets
4 skinless chicken breasts
2 Tbsp olive oil
2 Tbsp sesame seeds
A handful of finely chopped chives

Marinade
1 Tbsp honey
4 Tbsp brown sugar
125 ml (4 fl oz / 1/2 cup) light soy sauce
125 ml (4 fl oz / 1/2 cup) vegetable stock (page 134)
Juice of 1 lime
A handful of fresh or dried kaffir lime leaves

- Prepare marinade. Combine all ingredients in a pan and bring to the boil. Leave to boil until mixture has reduced by half, then remove from heat and discard kaffir lime leaves.
- Bring a pot of water to the boil. Cook cauliflower florets for about 12 minutes or until tender. Remove, drain and set aside.
- Heat oil in a frying pan over medium heat. Cook chicken breasts through and evenly on both sides. In the last minute of cooking, pour in three-quarters of marinade, coating the chicken with it. Remove and drain any residual liquid.
- Keeping pan heated, add cauliflower and pour remaining marinade over, coating the florets evenly before removing from heat.
- Garnish with sesame seeds and chives. Serve hot.

beef yakitori

Serves 4

Yakitori is a great way to savour and enjoy your meat, and the Japanese have it down pat. Recreate this experience in the comfort of your own kitchen!

450 g (1 lb) beef, fat trimmed and cut into cubes

8 spring onions (scallions), ends and leaves trimmed

Teriyaki Sauce

5 Tbsp Japanese soy sauce

4 Tbsp sake

1 Tbsp mirin

1 Tbsp castor (superfine) sugar

- Make teriyaki sauce. Combine all ingredients in a pan over medium heat. Leave to simmer until thickened, then remove from heat and set aside to cool.
- When sauce has cooled, place beef cubes in to marinade for 30 minutes or longer, if possible.
- Divide beef cubes equally among 4 skewers if serving as a starter, or 2 if for a main course, alternating them with spring onions. Grill for 5 minutes, turning skewers halfway through for even cooking.
- Serve immediately, with plain white rice if desired.

beef stew

Serves 4 to 6

Stew is the perfect comfort food to indulge in on a cold winter's night. I suggest making large portions of this stew and freezing it so you can have it whenever you feel like it!

4–6 brussel sprouts
2 Tbsp olive oil
Salt to taste
1 kg (2 lb 3 oz) lean beef cubes
3–6 cloves garlic, peeled and crushed
$1/2$ bottle of red wine
750 ml (24 fl oz / 3 cups) beef stock
4 carrots, peeled and sliced
12 button mushrooms, halved
2 zucchinis, sliced

- Prepare brussel sprouts. Bring a pot of water to the boil and boil them for 10 minutes. While boiling, preheat oven to 230°C (450°F). Remove brussel sprouts and drain well. Coat with a tablespoon of olive oil and season to taste. Roast in the oven for 20 minutes. When done, set aside.
- Heat remaining oil in a large pan or pot over medium-high heat. Stir-fry beef for 3–4 minutes, then add garlic and fry until fragrant.
- Add wine, then leave to simmer for 3–4 minutes before adding remaining ingredients. Cover pan or pot, reduce heat to low and leave to cook for 20–25 minutes. Beef should be fork-tender.
- Dish out and serve hot, or leave to cool, store in an airtight container and freeze until required.

new york strip steaks with red wine & pomegranate sauce

Serves 4

I made this dish quite by accident. I was shooting a promo for a show called *Weekend Kitchen*. They had a huge amount of food lined up for me to use. I started cooking the steak, then I saw these pomegranates and suddenly I had an inspiration. Their lovely tart flavour goes really well with the red wine sauce for this dish.

Olive oil

4 New York strip streaks, about 220 g (8 oz) each

4 cloves garlic, peeled and crushed

625 ml (20 fl oz / $2^{1}/_{2}$ cups) red wine

$^{1}/_{2}$ cup pomegranate seeds

- Heat a little olive oil in a pan over very high heat. Sear steaks for about 3–4 minutes on each side. This will seal its juices in. Remove from heat and set aside.

- Add more olive oil to pan and fry garlic for a minute. Add red wine, then leave to simmer for 2–3 minutes or until reduced. Return steak to pan, add pomegranate seeds and cook to desired doneness.

- If liked, serve with a bed of steamed spinach, which will soak up the flavour of the steak and red wine sauce nicely. Garnish as desired and serve immediately.

sesame steaks

Serves 4

I like to make this and eat it with a salad. This recipe is a beautiful example of Austral-Asian cuisine, as it's good, simple meat with an Oriental twist.

4 tenderloin steaks
4–6 Tbsp sesame seeds
2 Tbsp olive oil
Baby spinach leaves, or any preferred salad leaves

- Wrap steaks in cling film and place them on a flat work surface. Using a rolling pin, roll and press down on steaks to flatten them.
- Unwrap steaks and discard cling film. Coat with sesame seeds.
- Heat a little oil in a large, non-stick pan over high heat. Cook steaks for 2 minutes on each side for medium-rare doneness, or another minute if you prefer steaks to be well done.
- Slice steaks into thick strips and serve immediately on a bed of baby spinach or salad leaves.

venison steaks with red wine & mushroom sauce

Serves 4

Venison is such tender, delicious meat and it is a shame it is not cooked more in domestic kitchens. Just as good as beef or better, give this recipe a try when serving a fancy dinner.

4 venison steaks, about 220 g (8 oz) each

500 g (1 lb 1½ oz) spinach

1 Tbsp fresh chopped sage

Red Wine and Mushroom Sauce

2 Tbsp olive oil

6 shallots, peeled and finely chopped

20 button mushrooms, sliced in half

2 cloves garlic, peeled and crushed

4 fresh sage leaves

125 ml (4 fl oz / ½ cup) red wine

125 ml (4 fl oz / ½ cup) beef stock

Dressing

3–4 Tbsp sesame seeds

3 Tbsp dashi stock or vegetable stock (page 134)

1 tsp sugar

2 Tbsp soy sauce

1 Tbsp sesame oil + a little extra for spinach

- Prepare red wine and mushroom sauce. Heat 1 Tbsp oil in a saucepan over medium-high heat. Add shallots and cook for a minute before adding mushrooms. Cook for 2–3 minutes, then add garlic and sage and mix well. Add wine and stock and simmer until reduced by half. Remove from heat and set aside.

- Heat a large pan over high heat until very hot. Add remaining olive oil and sear venison steaks for 2 minutes. Reduce heat to medium and cook for another 4 minutes, then flip steaks over and cook for 6 minutes. Venison should be on the rare side. If you prefer them to be well done, turn off the heat, cover the pan and leave for 5 more minutes.

- Make dressing. In a non-stick pan over low heat, toast sesame seeds for 1–2 minutes. Leave a tablespoon aside for garnish and place the rest into a pestle and mortar. Grind until smooth. By the spoonful, mix stock, sugar, soy sauce and sesame oil. In a large wok or pan over medium heat, add a drizzle of sesame oil and throw in the spinach. Stir spinach continuously, cooking until the leaves wilt. Remove from heat and fold in the dressing.

- Divide spinach into 4 portions and press into your ramekin or timbale mould. Press firmly to compact spinach, place on a serving plate and lift it off to form a spinach timbale. Place steaks alongside spinach and spoon red wine and mushroom sauce over. Garnish with chopped sage and serve immediately.

lamb with wasabi crust

Serves 6 to 8

It's time to give the usual "lamb chops with mint sauce" a rest! This wasabi-crusted lamb is really something to serve when when you are craving for red meat with a kick.

1$\frac{1}{2}$ Tbsp wasabi powder

2 Tbsp water

1.5–2 kg (3–4 lb) racks of lamb, fat trimmed and carved into chops

- Mix wasabi powder and water together. Coat lamb chops evenly, then place in oven to cook. After 30 minutes, reduce temperature to 160°C (325°F) and cook for 1 hour.

- When done, remove lamb from oven and leave to cool for 15 minutes before serving.

herb-crusted rack of lamb with parsnip purée

Serves 4

It is hard to believe that this elegant dish is made with common everyday ingredients! The herb crust gives the lamb a fancy twist, and parsnip is an unusual but delicious substitute for potato as mash.

3 slices of white sandwich bread

3 Tbsp pine nuts

1 clove garlic, peeled and crushed

3 Tbsp olive oil

2 Tbsp fresh parsley

1 Tbsp fresh thyme

4 sun-dried tomatoes in oil

Salt for seasoning

Crushed black pepper for seasoning

1 kg (2 lb 3 oz) rack of lamb, fat trimmed and carved into chops

4 handfuls of spinach

Parsnip purée

5 medium-sized parsnips

3 Tbsp olive oil

- Preheat oven to 190°C (370°F).
- Using a blender, blend bread into fine crumbs, then add 2 Tbsp pine nuts, garlic, 2 Tbsp olive oil, herbs and sun-dried tomatoes and blend into a solid mixture. Season lamb chops with salt and pepper, then spread paste, covering the chops evenly. Roast chops in the oven for 20–25 minutes.
- Meanwhile, peel and chop parsnips. Bring a pot of water to the boil and boil parsnips for 15–20 minutes. Drain, then place in a blender with olive oil and blend until smooth. Set aside.
- In a large pan, heat remaining tablespoon of oil over medium heat. Stir-fry spinach quickly for 1–2 minutes, then add remaining pine nuts and remove from heat.
- Place a round pastry cutter on one corner of a serving plate. Fill with parsnip purée, then top with a quarter portion of spinach. Press down to compact mixture, then lift off the ring. Place lamb chops alongside and serve immediately.

seared foie gras with rocket leaves & figs

Serves 4

Many consider foie gras as a decadent treat that can hardly be classified as healthy eating, but believe it or not, foie gras is actually low in saturated fats! This is a treat worthy of its calories.

1 lobe of Grade A foie gras, about 1 lb (16 oz), cleaned

Rock salt

4 Tbsp of extra-virgin olive oil

4 fresh figs, cut into quarters.

4 large handfuls of rocket (arugula) leaves

Juice of 1 lemon

- Season foie gras with a little rock salt, then cut it into 4 pieces. Heat a pan over very high heat, until smoking hot. Sear foie gras for 30–40 seconds on each side. Remove from pan and set aside.

- In the same pan, heat a tablespoon of olive oil. Sear figs for 3–5 minutes or until caramelized.

- Dress rocket leaves with remaining olive oil, lemon juice and salt to taste. Divide leaves into equal portions on 4 serving plates together with figs. Place each piece of foie gras on top and serve immediately.

calf's liver on wasabi mash

Serves 4

A typical brassiere food, calf's liver, is making a comeback in top London restaurants. Instead of mustard, which is the traditional accompaniment, a silky-smooth wasabi mash is featured instead.

4 medium slices of calf's liver
2 medium onions, peeled and finely sliced
Olive oil
4 bunches of Chinese cabbage (*pak choy*)

Wasabi Mash

4–5 potatoes, peeled and quartered
4 tsp prepared wasabi paste
A handful of chopped spring onions
5 Tbsp of fresh milk
Salt to taste

- Start by making the mash. I usually prepare it in the morning of the day I need it, refrigerate it, then warm it up in the microwave. Bring a pot of water to the boil. Place potatoes in to cook until tender, for about 20–25 minutes.

- When ready, pop the potatoes into a potato dicer, if you have one, or drain water from the pot and shake it vigorously. Add wasabi paste and mix until smooth. Add spring onions, milk and salt to taste.

- Heat about 3 Tbsp oil in a pan over medium-high heat. Fry onions for 3–5 minutes, then reduce heat and cook for a further 5 minutes until onions are caramelised. Remove from pan and set aside.

- Bring a little water to the boil in a wok. Place the Chinese cabbage in a steaming container and place into wok, making sure the water does not go into the container. Steam for 3–5 minutes, then remove from heat and set aside.

- Reheat pan over very high heat until smoking hot. Sear liver for 1–2 minutes on each side to get medium-rare doneness, or just a minute if you want it rare. Serve liver immediately, with onions, steamed cabbage and mash on the side.

chopped liver

Serves 4

Chopped liver is a classic dish, but is often high in fat and cholesterol due to use of fat to bind the liver together. I've created a low-fat version that is just as delicious!

10 eggs
2 Tbsp olive oil
1 large onion, peeled and sliced
1 lb (450 g) chicken livers
6–8 slices white sandwich bread
A handful of chopped parsley

- Hard-boil all the eggs and set aside. Heat a tablespoon of olive oil in a large pan. Fry onions for 3–5 minutes, stirring continuously. Add chicken livers and cook for around 3–4 minutes. Do not overcook or livers will be tough.

- Transfer liver and onions to a blender and blend well. Peel hard-boiled eggs. Add 6 whole eggs and just the whites of 2 eggs. Set remaining 2 eggs aside. Blend to a slightly chunky consistency.

- Toast bread, then cut out rounds using a round pastry cutter. To serve, place cutter on a serving plate and spoon liver in until full. Lift cutter off, then place a round of toast on top. Grate remaining 2 eggs and place on the side, together with some chopped parsley.

fish & seafood

Hailbut with Sun-dried Tomato Sauce 95

Seabass Nicoise 96

Sashimi Tuna Wraps 98

Seared Tuna on Parsnip Purée 100

Salmon with Wasabi Pea Crust 102

Surf and Turf 104

Tiger Prawns with Avocado & Salmon Roe in Orange Vinaigrette 106

Miso Prawns 108

Steamed Clams in Wine 110

Crab with Salmon Roe 112

Vodka Lobster 114

Lobster Tail with Asparagus 116

Marinated Octopus 118

This simple seafood dish is redolent with the glorious flavours of the Mediterranean. The tomato sauce can also be used for bruschetta when serving canapés, or as a dip with vegetable sticks.

halibut with sun-dried tomato sauce

Serves 4

4 halibut fillets, about 175 g (6 oz) each
A pinch of salt
A pinch of ground white pepper

Sun-dried Tomato Sauce

6 plum tomatoes, seeded
250 g (9 oz) sun-dried tomatoes in olive oil, drained
1 clove garlic, peeled
Juice of 1 lemon
$1/2$ small red chilli
A handful of fresh basil leaves
1 Tbsp olive oil

- Skin fillets, if preferred, or leave intact. Place them on a baking tray and season well with salt and pepper. Preheat oven to 180°C (350°F).

- Make sun-dried tomato sauce. Place tomatoes, sun-dried tomatoes, garlic, lemon juice, chilli, olive oil and basil in a blender and blend until roughly chopped. Spoon mixture over fillets, then place in the oven to cook for 18–20 minutes.

- Remove from heat and serve immediately.

seabass nicoise

Serves 4

Nicoise salad originated from France and has been a classic salad on the menu since. Here, the classic nicoise vegetables are cooked with a wonderful whole seabass. It's a great dish to have on a fine summer's night, with white wine.

6 new potatoes, cut into quarters

$3/4$ cup olive oil

$3/4$ cup lemon juice

4 whole sea bass, about 1–1$1/2$ lb (450–500 g) each, scaled and cleaned

30 French beans

14–18 black olives, pitted

12–14 Sun-blushed Tomatoes (page 135)

55 g (2 oz) canned anchovies, drained

Salt to taste

Crushed black pepper to taste

A desired amount of fresh chopped parsley

- Bring a pot of water to the boil. Blanch potatoes for 5 minutes, then remove, drain and set aside.
- Preheat oven to 220°C (44°F). In a large, deep baking tray, mix oil and lemon juice, then place fish in the centre of tray. Add potatoes, beans, olives, tomatoes and anchovies, scattering them over fish. Season with salt and pepper, then place in oven for 40 minutes or until fish is fork-tender and juices run clear.
- Garnish with fresh parsley and serve immediately, with some bread to mop up all the lovely gravy.

sashimi tuna wraps

Serves 4

I had this in a very trendy London club during a private party, and I loved it as for a canapé or starter because it was carb-free. Addictively tasty, these will be snatched off the plate in no time at all!

1 large tuna steak, about 250–300 g (9–11 oz)
A handful of fresh rocket leaves

Dipping Sauce
2 Tbsp lemon juice
2 Tbsp sesame oil
2 Tbsp soy sauce

- Heat a non-stick pan until very hot, then sear tuna for 30 seconds on each side. Remove from heat and leave aside to cool on a chopping board.
- Make dipping sauce. Combine lemon juice, sesame oil and soy sauce and mix well. Set aside.
- Slice tuna steak into $1/2$-cm ($1/4$-in) thick slices. Place some rocket leaves on each slice, then roll them up so that tuna wraps the leaves.
- Serve immediately, with dipping sauce on the side.

seared tuna on parsnip purée

Serves 4 to 6

You really do not need the cheese and butter in a dish like this— the tuna is immensely flavourful with just a little seasoning. This is great as a light lunch or starter.

1 bulb of garlic
8 large parsnips
6–8 Tbsp olive oil
450 g (1 lb) tuna steak, cut into 4 pieces
A pinch of rock salt

- Place garlic in a square of aluminium foil. Drizzle 1–1$\frac{1}{2}$ Tbsp olive oil over, wrap the entire bulb and place in oven to roast at 230°C (450°F) for 40-50 minutes.
- While garlic is roasting, peel parsnips and chop off their ends. Chop further into wedges. Bring a pot of water to the boil and boil parsnips for 15–20 minutes or until tender.
- While parsnips are cooking, heat about 1 Tbsp olive oil in a non-stick pan or wok over high heat. Sear tuna steaks for 30 seconds on each side, then remove and set aside.
- When parsnips are tender, drain and transfer to a blender. Add rock salt, remaining olive oil and 3 cloves of roasted garlic (skin discarded) and blend until smooth.
- Divide parsnip purée among 4 serving plates. Place tuna on top and scatter remaining cloves of roasted garlic. Serve immediately.

salmon with wasabi pea crust

Serves 4 to 6

Wasabi-flavoured peas are great as a snack, and I remember how they were all the rage when they first came out. They were served alongside drinks in hip, trendy bars. I've found another use for them in this really simple salmon recipe!

1 cup wasabi-flavoured peas
4 salmon fillets, 250 g (9 oz) each
Olive oil

- Using a pestle and mortar, crush wasabi peas almost to a powder. Alternatively, place peas in a plastic bag, seal and crush with a heavy rolling pin. Spread crushed peas out on a plate.
- Coat salmon fillets with crushed peas. Heat a little olive oil in a frying pan over high heat and sear fillets for 2 minutes on each side. Do not overcook or the wasabi pea crust will burn.
- Serve immediately.

surf and turf

Serves 4

This was a hip menu item back in the USA in the 1970s. Never mind its reputation for being culinary kitsch; It doesn't pay to be a food snob, and I do love a meat and seafood combination once in a while!

4 tenderloin steaks (filet mignon)

Crushed black pepper

4 small lobster tails, flesh removed from shell

3–4 Tbsp extra virgin olive oil

Lemon juice 1 Tbsp or to taste

A pinch or two of rock salt

Mixed salad leaves, enough for 4 people

A few spoonfuls of salmon roe (optional)

Avocado Sauce

Juice of 1 lemon

5 Tbsp water

2 ripe avocados, peeled and pitted

Fresh basil leaves

- Make avocado sauce. Combine lemon juice, water, avocado flesh and basil leaves in a food processor and blend until smooth. Set aside. Preheat oven to 190°C (375°F).
- Season steaks with pepper. Heat a griddle pan on very high heat for 1–2 minutes. Sear steaks for 1–2 minutes on each side, then transfer to oven and cook for 10 minutes.
- Meanwhile, using the same griddle pan, sear lobster tails for 2–3 minutes on each side. Remove from heat and drizzle with a little olive oil, lemon juice and salt.
- Toss salad leaves in remaining lemon juice, olive oil and salt. Divide among 4 serving plates, followed by steaks and lobster tails. Dish out avocado sauce and salmon roe on the side, if using. Serve immediately.

tiger prawns with avocado & salmon roe in orange vinaigrette

Serves 4

I must confess; I replicated this recipe. A few years back, when I was the guest chef at the Shangri-la hotel in Bangkok, it was one of the items on the buffet that I really enjoyed! Even my daughter loves it, and the first time she tried it was at the ripe old age of two years! The orange vinaigrette really complements the fresh seafood flavour of the prawns and roe, and the creamy avocado presents a soothing finish to temper the liveliness of the flavours.

450 g (1 lb) tiger prawns

1 orange

1 Tbsp djion mustard

½ clove garlic, peeled and crushed

½ cup olive oil

juice of ½ lemon

1–2 avocados, peeled, pitted and chopped

4 spring onions (scallions), chopped

100 g (3½ oz) salmon roe

- Poach prawns in boiling water for 3–5 minutes or until prawns turn pink. Remove prawns, drain and set aside.
- Squeeze orange for juice into a mixing bowl and scoop out some of its flesh. Mix in mustard, garlic, olive oil and lemon juice.
- Add prawns and avocados and toss well. Sprinkle chopped spring onions and salmon roe over and serve immediately.

miso prawns

Serves 4

Miso has got to be one of my favourite Japanese flavours. It goes so well with other ingredients such as garlic, lemon and even honey, as demonstrated in quick, simple dish. Serve this up for a Japanese-inspired meal.

Olive oil

700 g (1½ lb) prawns, peeled and deveined

A handful of fresh coriander (cilantro) leaves

A handful of chopped spring onions

Marinade

1 Tbsp grated fresh ginger

1 clove garlic, peeled and crushed

2–3 Tbsp honey

1 Tbsp miso paste

Juice of 1 large lemon

- In a mixing bowl, mix marinade ingredients well and set aside.

- In a large pan, heat a little olive oil over high heat. Cook prawns for a few minutes or until they turn pink. Pour in marinade and toss prawns to ensure they are well coated, then remove from heat.

- Arrange prawns over coriander leaves and garnish with spring onions. Drizzle with remaining marinade and serve immediately.

steamed clams in wine

Serves 4

I love steamed clams or mussels, but unfortunately many restaurants like to add cream and butter to emulsify the dish. My version sees the clams flavoured with garlic and fresh herbs, spiked with a little white wine, and made succulent due to the stock and sweet steaming juices that come from steaming the clams. Serve with some crusty white bread on the side to mop up the lovely clear broth.

2 Tbsp olive oil

4 shallots, peeled and finely chopped

3 cloves garlic, peeled and crushed

900 g (2 lb) of clams

$1/2$ cup dry white wine

2 cups fish stock (page 134)

A handful of fresh tarragon or basil leaves

- Heat 1 Tbsp olive oil in a big saucepan over medium-high heat. Add shallots and garlic and fry for 1 minute before adding clams and wine. Clams should begin to open after 1–2 minutes.

- Add stock, cover pan and leave to simmer for 5 minutes. Discard any unopened clams and throw fresh herbs in. Drizzle remaining spoonful of olive oil over.

- Dish out and serve immediately.

crab with salmon roe

Serves 4

I adore salmon eggs and never tire of them; to me, they are as good as caviar. This dish goes really well with bubbly, and makes a tasty, elegant starter, and you can throw this together in a matter of minutes!

370 g (13 oz) fresh or premium canned crab meat
Salt to taste
Crushed black pepper to taste
Juice of 1 lemon
2 large tomatoes, seeded and finely diced
1 Tbsp olive oil
4 Tbsp avocado sauce (page 104)
4 Tbsp salmon roe
Herb oil (page 136)

- In a mixing bowl, season crab with salt and pepper. Add lemon juice and mix well. Add diced tomatoes, followed by olive oil. Mix well.
- To serve, place a round pastry cutter on a serving plate. Pack crab mixture tightly into ring, pressing down firmly to compact it. Gently lift off cutter, then drizzle a tablespoon of avocado sauce over and spoon some salmon roe on top of crab.

vodka lobster

Serves 4

The vodka adds a clean, sharp finish to this chic interpretation of a seafood starter. Needless to say, double your servings as your guests will be sure to ask for seconds!

Olive oil
1 small white onion, peeled and finely sliced
1 clove garlic, peeled
Medium-size tomatoes, seeded and finely chopped
450 g (1 lb) fresh lobster meat, coarsely chopped
125 ml (4 fl oz / $1/2$ cup) vodka
Salt to taste
Crushed black pepper to taste
Juice of 1 lemon
A handful of fresh dill, roughly chopped

- Heat a little olive oil in a frying pan over medium heat and fry onion. Add garlic, followed by tomatoes and stir well. Add lobster meat and cook for 2–3 minutes, stirring continuously. Remove from heat and set aside.

- In a stainless steel pan, add vodka and heat over a flame for 30 seconds. Let the vodka catch fire and immediately pour over lobster. Flambé ingredients until the flames die down. Remove from heat and season with salt and pepper.

- Divide lobster among martini glasses or wine glasses. Add lemon juice and dill to each serving and serve immediately.

lobster tail with asparagus

Serves 4

Simple, elegant and not too fussy. I love lobster for its sweet succulence, and think you need to do little with it other than to make sure that you do not overcook it, which will result in stringy, dry lobster flesh.

4 lobster tails

1 Tbsp olive oil

Rock salt

16 large asparagus spears

2 cloves garlic, peeled and crushed

Chopped chives for garnish

Dipping Sauce

Juice of 2 lemons

Juice of one orange

4 Tbsp light soy sauce

- Make dipping sauce. Heat lemon juice, orange juice and soy sauce in a small saucepan and bring to a simmer until mixture reduces by a third.
- Season lobster tails with salt and olive oil. Heat a griddle pan over very high heat, then sear on both sides. Reduce heat to medium and leave to cook for 3–5 minutes on each side. Remove from heat and set aside. If preferred, remove meat from the shells, or run a sharp knife down the back of each shell and leave as is.
- Heat a little olive oil in a wok over high heat. Fry asparagus for 3–5 minutes, and add garlic in the last minute of cooking.
- Serve lobster and asparagus immediately, garnished with chives, and with dipping sauce on the side.

marinated octopus

Serves 4

Marinated octopus is originally an Italian dish, but can be found in restaurants all over the world today. I love this dish for its subtle flavours.

700 g (1½ lb) baby octopus, cleaned
1 large carrot, peeled and cut into matchsticks
6 Tbsp olive oil
Juice of 1 lemon
2 cloves garlic, peeled and crushed
A small handful of chives, chopped

- Bring a large pan of water to the boil. Cook the octopus for 4–5 minutes, then remove, drain and set aside.
- Place carrot in a mixing bowl and add the olive oil, lemon juice, garlic and chives.
- Drain the octopus and add to the bowl. Toss well and serve immediately.

desserts

Lemon & Olive Oil Ice Cream 121

Mango & Green Tea Sorbet 122

Vanilla Yoghurt with Meringue & Berries 124

Passion Fruit Soufflé 126

Grilled Bananas & Marshmallows 128

Apricot Compote 130

Without overdoing the cream and sugar, this ice cream is a real treat for a hot day, as it is refreshing without being cloying and heavy.

lemon & olive oil ice cream

Serves 4 as a starter

½ cup extra-virgin olive oil

1 lemon, grated for zest

Juice of 2 lemons

1⅓ cups low-fat (skim) milk

½ cup sugar

A pinch of salt

1 cup heavy (double) cream

6 large egg yolks

- In a small pan, warm olive oil over low heat. Add lemon zest, then remove from heat and leave aside for the flavours to infuse and develop.
- In a pot, combine milk, sugar and salt and warm over medium heat until the sugar and salt are well dissolved and the milk is warm. Stir occasionally to prevent mixture from scorching, and do not allow it to boil.
- While milk is heating, place cream in a large bowl and place ice in a bigger bowl to make an ice bath. Place bowl with cream over ice and set aside.
- Separate egg yolks from whites. Place yolks in a medium-sized bowl and give them a quick whisk. Add warm milk mixture, about a ½ cup at a time, whisking as you add it. When all the milk is incorporated, return mixture to pot. Return it to heat, whisking constantly until mixture thickens and coats the back of a spoon. Ensure it does not scorch.
- Strain mixture through a fine-mesh wire strainer over the heavy cream and stir to mix. Add lemon-infused olive oil and lemon juice and whisk until smooth. Leave mixture to cool to room temperature.
- Cover bowl and freeze mixture until firm before serving. If liked, garnish with some sprigs of fresh rosemary.

mango & green tea sorbet

Serves 4

This unusual combination of flavours come together in the best of ways; the sweetness of the mangoes is accentuated by the slight bitterness of green tea. All in all, it's a fantastic way to end a heavy meal as it refreshes the palate!

$2/3$ cup water

$1/3$ cup of loose green tea leaves

$1/2$ cup sugar

3 ripe mangoes

3 Tbsp fresh lemon juice

- Combine water and tea leaves in a saucepan. Bring just to the boil, then remove from heat and let it stand for 5 minutes. Strain, discarding leaves.
- Transfer tea mixture to a saucepan, add sugar and bring to the boil for 1 minute or until sugar dissolves. Remove from heat and leave to cool for about 30 minutes.
- While tea is cooling, peel mangoes and cut flesh into small pieces. Place in a blender or food processor, add lemon juice and blend into a purée. Add tea and blend until smooth.
- Transfer mixture to a plastic container or deep cake tin and freeze for at least 3 hours.

vanilla yoghurt with meringues & berries

Serves 4 to 6

A light, sweet dessert like this practically effortless to throw together. Any mix of sweet, tart berries can be used, and using store-bought meringues cuts down the preparation time, and makes it a whole lot easier.

4 cups plain, non-fat yoghurt

1 tsp vanilla extract

3 Tbsp castor (superfine) sugar

2 dozen store-bought mini meringues

450 g (1 lb) mixed fresh berries

- In a mixing bowl, combine yoghurt, vanilla extract and sugar and mix well.
- Using your hands, crush about $3/4$ of meringues over yoghurt, adding berries after. Mix well.
- Serve with remaining whole meringues on the side. Garnish with more berries if desired. Yoghurt can also be frozen before serving.

passion fruit soufflé

Serves 4

This fat-free soufflé is not as difficult to make as it seems; there are only three ingredients involved! I love the tangy, tart flavour of passion fruit and this is but one of the many ways to serve it in dessert.

6 egg whites
2 Tbsp castor (superfine) sugar
6 passion fruit

- Whisk egg whites until stiff peaks form, then whisk in sugar to make a meringue.

- Cut open passion fruit and scoop out their pulp. Mix it in with meringue, then divide among 4 ramekins. Bake for 10 minutes or until soufflés rise and are light brown.

- Remove from oven and serve immediately.

grilled bananas & marshmallows

Serves 4 to 6

This dessert will take you back to your memories of camping out in the wild and toasting marshmallows by an open fire. Choose bananas that are just ripe and not overripe ones, in case they become too mushy while cooking.

2 bananas, peeled and sliced into 2.5-cm (1-in) slices
6–8 marshmallows, sliced into halves
1 Tbsp olive oil

- Heat oil in a pan over high heat. Cook banana slices for a few minutes, then add marshmallow halves and cook until they melt.

- Heat oil in a pan over high heat. Cook banana slices for a few minutes, then add marshmallow halves and cook until they begin to melt.

- Remove from pan and transfer to a serving plate. Serve immediately.

apricot compote

Serves 4

This light dessert is the perfect finish to any meal, and never goes out of style. If you like, serve with some low-fat yoghurt or ice cream.

2 Tbsp olive oil

2 Tbsp castor (superfine) sugar

450 g (1 lb) ripe apricots, pitted and cut into quarters

- Heat olive oil in a pan. Add sugar, allowing the granules to dissolve and turn the colour of caramel.
- Add apricots to pan and leave to simmer over low heat, covered, for 8–10 minutes. Add a little water, if needed.
- Transfer apricots and liquid to a blender and blend until fine. Pour into a container and leave to cool.
- Serve chilled.

Daniel Green launches his TV Program "Healthy Eating with Daniel Green" and "World Dining with Daniel Green" which will be broadcast over six cities in Asia.

Green's menu planner

Whatever the occasion, be it a simple dinner with your family or a get-together with good friends, here are some ways in which you can match the recipes in this book together, to create a sumptuous (yet healthy) spread that will have your family and friends craving for more!

For The Connoisseur

Scallops in Red Wine
Pasta with Trio of Mushrooms
Lemon & Olive Oil Ice Cream

For A Special Occasion

Vodka Lobster
Lamb with Wasabi Crust
Passion Fruit Soufflé

A Japanese Encounter

Japanese Tuna Tartare
Miso Prawns
Mango & Green Tea Ice Cream

For The Vegetarian

Asparagus Raft
Green's Energiser
Vanilla Yoghurt with Meringue and Berries

France At Home

Soup de Poisson
Seabass Nicoise
Vanilla Yoghurt with Meringue and Berries

basic recipes

Vegetable Stock
Makes about 625 ml (20 fl oz / 2$\frac{1}{2}$ cups)

Making your own stock need not be a chore. This vegetable stock is easy to make and you'll see for yourself the difference in the taste alone.

2 carrots, chopped
2 onions, peeled and quartered
2 celery sticks, chopped
$\frac{1}{2}$ fennel bulb, chopped
Stalk from a head of broccoli, chopped
4 large tomatoes
8 button mushrooms, halved
6 black peppercorns
1 bay leaf
4 Tbsp tomato paste
3 parsley stalks
1 litre (32 fl oz / 4 cups) water

- Place all ingredients in a large pot and simmer for about 50 minutes. Strain the stock before use.

Chicken Stock
Makes about 625 ml (20 fl oz / 2$\frac{1}{2}$ cups)

The key to a good low-fat chicken stock is to refrigerate it, then skim off the fat from the surface. Homemade stocks can be stored in the refrigerator for 2–3 days and up to a month in the freezer.

1 medium chicken, cut into 8 pieces
6 button mushrooms, halved
$\frac{1}{2}$ tsp salt
1 tsp black peppercorns
2 carrots, chopped
2 onions, peeled and quartered
2 celery sticks, chopped
3 garlic cloves
4 large tomatoes
3 parsley stalks
1 litre (32 fl oz / 4 cups) water

- Place all ingredients in a large pot and simmer for about 50 minutes.
- Strain the stock, then leave to cool and refrigerate for about 1 hour.
- Remove the layer of fat from the surface of stock using a large metal spoon.
- Reheat the stock and use as required.

Fish Stock
Makes about 625 ml (20 fl oz / 2$\frac{1}{2}$ cups)

This is another stock that can be prepared without fuss.

6 large tiger prawns
Trimmings (heads, skin and bones) of 4 medium size fish (sea bass or salmon)
2 carrots, chopped
2 onions, peeled and quartered
2 celery sticks, chopped
3 garlic cloves
4 large tomatoes
4 Tbsp tomato paste
3 parsley stalks
1 litre (32 fl oz / 4 cups) water

- Place all ingredients in a large pot and simmer for about 50 minutes. Strain the stock before use.

Sun-blushed Tomatoes

Serves 4

This is a way of having the texture and taste of sun-dried tomatoes, but without the intense flavour sun-dried tomatoes normally have. Perfect as a side for main dishes or in salads.

24 plum tomatoes
85 ml (24/ fl oz / ¾ cup) olive oil
Salt to taste
Pepper to taste

- Cut tomatoes into quarters, then place In a large deep baking tray.
- Pour olive oil over and season well with salt and pepper.
- Place in an oven preheated at 160°C (325°F) for 30 minutes, then turn off heat and leave tomatoes for another 30 minutes.
- To store, place them in airtight jar and pour in enough olive oil to cover. They will keep up to a week at room temperature, and up to 1 month refrigerated.

Tomato Drizzle
Makes about 220 g (8 oz)

This gives a vibrant hue to any dish.

1 can chopped tomatoes, about 220 g (8 oz)
4 Tbsp extra-virgin olive oil

- Combine all ingredients in a blender or food processor. Pour dressing into an airtight container and refrigerate for up to 2 weeks.

Herb Oil
Makes about 250 ml (8 fl oz / 1 cup)

This keeps well when refrigerated, and makes a stylish garnish for your dishes.

250 ml (8 fl oz / 1 cup) extra-virgin olive oil
A handful of fresh Italian basil
A pinch of salt
A pinch of crushed black pepper

- Combine ingredients in a blender or food processor. Pour dressing into an airtight container and refrigerate for up to 2 weeks.

Fusion Salad Dressing
Makes about 3 cups

This dressing combines the best of both Italian and Japanese flavours.

1 Tbsp Dijon mustard
2 limes, squeezed for juice
85 ml (2 fl oz / $1/4$ cup) light soy sauce
250 ml (8 fl oz / 1 cup) extra virgin olive oil
1 garlic clove, crushed
4 Tbsp sesame oil
2.5-cm (1-in) fresh ginger, peeled and grated

- Combine all ingredients well, then leave aside to marinate for 30 minutes before use. Pour dressing into an airtight container and refrigerate for up to to 1 week.

Wasabi Drizzle

Makes about 250 g (9 oz)

This piquant dressing gives punch and kick to regular dishes!

250 g (1 cup) non-fat plain yoghurt
Salt to taste
Pepper to taste
3 Tbsp Wasabi paste
1 lime, squeezed for juice
1 Tbsp chopped fresh coriander (cilantro) leaves

- Combine ingredients in a blender or food processor. Pour dressing into an airtight container and refrigerate for up to 1 week.

Full name : Daniel Green
Nickname : Dan
Birthday : September 1, 1970
Hometown : London

Years as a Television Host, Presenter & Celebrity Chef: 1999–present.

Present career: Host at ShopNBC since 2004. I do every product category but I specialise in cooking.

Favorite color: Black. It is so easy and always looks smart. I am from London. Like New York, we are afraid of colour.

Favorite hobbies: Cooking every day. Traveling to Asia.

Favorite food: Thai. I have been to Thailand over 30 times, and I love it so much that I have even written a cookbook on Thai food!

More About Me

As a child, I really enjoyed…tennis, cooking and being a spoilt younger brother.

How I got into the home shopping business…I hosted cooking and travel shows in the UK and started doing some work in the USA. My agent asked me what I thought about shopping TV and I was thrilled at the chance to explore it.

The best part about being a ShopNBC host is…live TV. It changes all the time. Good or bad, it is always so exciting.

My favorite on-air moments are…Always when it involves laughing!

My most embarrassing moment on air… Well I said something I shouldn't, but it was funny. I also almost burnt down the house I was doing a live cooking show in, on UK TV.

The most challenging part of hosting is… I enjoy it so much I really can't think of it as being challenging.

Off camera, I…am the same person. You can't perform on live TV. You have to be yourself.

My greatest achievement…is writing my first cookbook. I was quite taken away when I saw it for the first time. Then on the third page it said "To Eleanor with love." (that's my daughter.) Needless to say I got teary-eyed.

I am known as The Model Cook…because after I lost weight around 18 years ago I went into modeling for a few years. It was fun but not a career I wanted to follow. Then I ended up cooking to lose weight, and here I am!

My food…is not intended for a diet. I simply lower the fat content in the dishes I love to eat. This way, I hope to help people be better able to manage their weight by eating healthily.

I spend my free time…with my wife and daughter as much as possible. I do love to travel too.

In my personal life, I am motivated by… my parents and my family. I just want to bring up my daughter with the same values that my wife and I share.

My mentors are…a brilliant director Stephen Daldry who has great success in his career but possesses such modesty. On a personal level, my wife Jane. She always reminds me of what's real and makes the right choices all the time.

My friends and family would describe me as…someone does not take himself too seriously, and who is always looking for a way to make people laugh.

My hidden talents are…in fishing. But sadly, I don't get much of a chance to do so nowadays.

The accomplishment I am most proud of… is making my dream to be on TV one day happen.

I always look forward to…spending time with my wife and daughter.

If I wasn't hosting cooking shows, the career path I'd have followed would be…still something in in the form of cooking and travel. I've always had a passion for the two.

I am really bad at this, but wish I was great at…singing. I would love to be able to sing, and I am really, really bad. Even the cats leave the room when I sing!

weights & measures

Quantities for this book are given in Metric and American (spoon and cup) measures. Standard spoon and cup measurements used are: 1 teaspoon = 5 ml, 1 tablespoon = 15 ml, 1 cup = 250 ml. All measures are level unless otherwise stated.

Liquid & Volume Measures

Metric	Imperial	American
5 ml	$^1/_6$ fl oz	1 teaspoon
10 ml	$^1/_3$ fl oz	1 dessertspoon
15 ml	$^1/_2$ fl oz	1 tablespoon
60 ml	2 fl oz	$^1/_4$ cup (4 tablespoons)
85 ml	$2^1/_2$ fl oz	$^1/_3$ cup
90 ml	3 fl oz	$^3/_8$ cup (6 tablespoons)
125 ml	4 fl oz	$^1/_2$ cup
180 ml	6 fl oz	$^3/_4$ cup
250 ml	8 fl oz	1 cup
300 ml	10 fl oz ($^1/_2$ pint)	$1^1/_4$ cups
375 ml	12 fl oz	$1^1/_2$ cups
435 ml	14 fl oz	$1^3/_4$ cups
500 ml	16 fl oz	2 cups
625 ml	20 fl oz (1 pint)	$2^1/_2$ cups
750 ml	24 fl oz ($1^1/_5$ pints)	3 cups
1 litre	32 fl oz ($1^3/_5$ pints)	4 cups
1.25 litres	40 fl oz (2 pints)	5 cups
1.5 litres	48 fl oz ($2^2/_5$ pints)	6 cups
2.5 litres	80 fl oz (4 pints)	10 cups

Dry Measures

Metric	Imperial
30 grams	1 ounce
45 grams	$1^1/_2$ ounces
55 grams	2 ounces
70 grams	$2^1/_2$ ounces
85 grams	3 ounces
100 grams	$3^1/_2$ ounces
110 grams	4 ounces
125 grams	$4^1/_2$ ounces
140 grams	5 ounces
280 grams	10 ounces
450 grams	16 ounces (1 pound)
500 grams	1 pound, $1^1/_2$ ounces
700 grams	$1^1/_2$ pounds
800 grams	$1^3/_4$ pounds
1 kilogram	2 pounds, 3 ounces
1.5 kilograms	3 pounds, $4^1/_2$ ounces
2 kilograms	4 pounds, 6 ounces

Oven Temperature

	°C	°F	Gas Regulo
Very slow	120	250	1
Slow	150	300	2
Moderately slow	160	325	3
Moderate	180	350	4
Moderately hot	190/200	370/400	5/6
Hot	210/220	410/440	6/7
Very hot	230	450	8
Super hot	250/290	475/550	9/10

Length

Metric	Imperial
0.5 cm	$^1/_4$ inch
1 cm	$^1/_2$ inch
1.5 cm	$^3/_4$ inch
2.5 cm	1 inch

index of recipes

Desserts

Apricot Compote 130
Grilled Bananas & Marshmallows 128
Lemon & Olive Oil Ice Cream 121
Mango & Green Tea Sorbet 122
Passion Fruit Soufflé 126
Vanilla Yoghurt with Meringue & Berries 124

Fish

Green Tea Noodles with Salmon & Avocado Mousse 70
Hailbut with Sun-dried Tomato Sauce 95
Japanese Tuna Tartare 16
Salmon with Wasabi Pea Crust 102
Sashimi Tuna Wraps 98
Seabass Nicoise 96
Seared Tuna on Parsnip Purée 100

Meat & Poultry

Beef Stew 76
Beef Yakitori 74
Calf's Liver on Wasabi Mash 92
Chicken with Kaffir Lime Leaf & Cauliflower 73
Chopped Liver 92
Egg Noodles with Chicken & Vegetables 66
Lamb with Wasabi Crust 84
New York Strip Steaks with Red Wine & Pomegranate Sauce 78
Herb-crusted Rack of Lamb with Parsnip Purée 86
Seared Foie Gras with Rocket Leaves & Figs 88
Sesame Steaks 80
Surf and Turf 108
Venison Steaks with Red Wine & Mushroom Sauce 82

Noodles & Pasta

Egg Noodles with Chicken & Vegetables 66
Green Tea Noodles with Salmon & Avocado Mousse 70
Pasta with Trio of Mushrooms 57
Sesame Soba Noodles 64
Shanghai Noodles 62
Soba Noodle Soup 68

Rice

Edamame Risotto 60
Truffle Risotto 58

Seafood

Crab & Avocado Tower 12
Crab with Salmon Roe 112
Lobster Tail with Asparagus 116
Marinated Octopus 118
Miso Prawns 108
Prawn with Tomato Coulis 22
Salmon & Avocado Wrap 18
Spicy Chilli Calamari 14
Steamed Clams in Wine 112
Surf and Turf 104
Tiger Prawns with Avocado & Salmon Roe in Orange Vinaigrette 106
Vodka Lobster 114

Side Dishes

Green's Energiser 42
Roasted Baby Aubergines 44
Roasted Edamame with Garlic 46
Roasted Vegetables 48
Sun-dried Tomato Mash 54
Wasabi Mash 52

Soups

Soup de Poisson 36
Sweet Corn & Lemon Grass Soup 40
Tomato & Basil Soup 38

Starters & Appetisers

Bean Curd Guacamole 24
Bread Dips, Two Flavours 32
Caesar Salad 28
Crab & Avocado Tower 12
Japanese Tuna Tartare 16
Prawn with Tomato Coulis 22
Salad with Everything 30
Salad with Pumpkin Seeds 26
Salmon and Avocado Wrap 18
Soup de Poisson 36
Spicy Chilli Calamari 14
Sweet Corn & Lemon Grass Soup 40
Taboule 50
Tomato & Basil Soup 38

Vegetables & Salads

Asparagus Raft 34
Bean Curd Guacamole 24
Caesar Salad 28
Green's Energiser 42
Pasta with Trio of Mushrooms 57
Roasted Baby Aubergines 44
Roasted Edamame with Garlic 46
Roasted Vegetables 48
Salad with Everything 30
Salad with Pumpkin Seeds 26
Sun-dried Tomato Mash 54
Taboule 50
Wasabi Mash 52

International TV Personality, Chef & Author—
Daniel Green, The Model Cook